Three's A Crowd

ate

These trios can be performed with any other combination of instruments within Book 2.

Brass

A mix and match collection of 19 trio arrangements by James Power.

CHESTER MUSIC

London/New York/Paris/Sydney/Copenhagen/Berlin/Madrid/Tokyo

Contents

Published by
Chester Music
14/15 Berners Street, London W1T 3LJ, England.

Exclusive Distributors:

Music Sales Limited
Distribution Centre, Newmarket Road, Bury St Edmunds,
Suffolk IP33 3YB, England,

Music Sales Corporation
257 Park Avenue South, New York, NY 10010,
United States of America.

Music Sales Pty Limited
120 Rothschild Avenue, Rosebery, NSW 2018, Australia.

Order No. PM189824R
ISBN 0-7119-9379-3
This book © Copyright 2003 Chester Music
No part of this publication may be copied or reproduced in any form or by any
means including photocopying without prior permission from Chester Music.

The instruments featured on the cover were provided by
Macari's Musical Instruments, London.
Models provided by Truly Scrumptious and Norrie Carr.
Photography by George Taylor.
Printed in the United Kingdom.

Greensleeves

Traditional English

Grandfather's Clock

Traditional

The Entertainer

Scott Joplin (1868-1917)

The Yellow Rose Of Texas

Traditional American

Für Elise

Ludwig van Beethoven (1770-1827)

Allegro

Wolfgang Amadeus Mozart (1756-1791)

Con Moto

The Big Brass Band

James Power

12

B

To CODA ⊕

D.S. al CODA ⊕

⊕ **CODA**

A French Frolic

Traditional

O Come All Ye Faithful

Traditional Christmas Song

Ding Dong Merrily On High

Traditional Christmas Song

17

Ecossaise

Ludwig van Beethoven (1770-1827)

Buffalo Gals

Traditional American

Rag Doll

James Power

C

To CODA ⊕   **D.S. al CODA ⊕**

⊕ CODA

Bill Bailey

Traditional American

Traditional Tunes Of Scotland

Traditional

Radetsky March

Johann Strauss I (1804-1849)

Minuet

Wolfgang Amadeus Mozart (1756-1791)

Dance Of The Little Swans

Pyotr Ilyich Tchaikovsky (1840-1893)

Pyramids

Timing and tuning exercise

5/07 (62307)